# Habitats Infographics

## By Harriet Brundle

Designed by Charlotte Neve

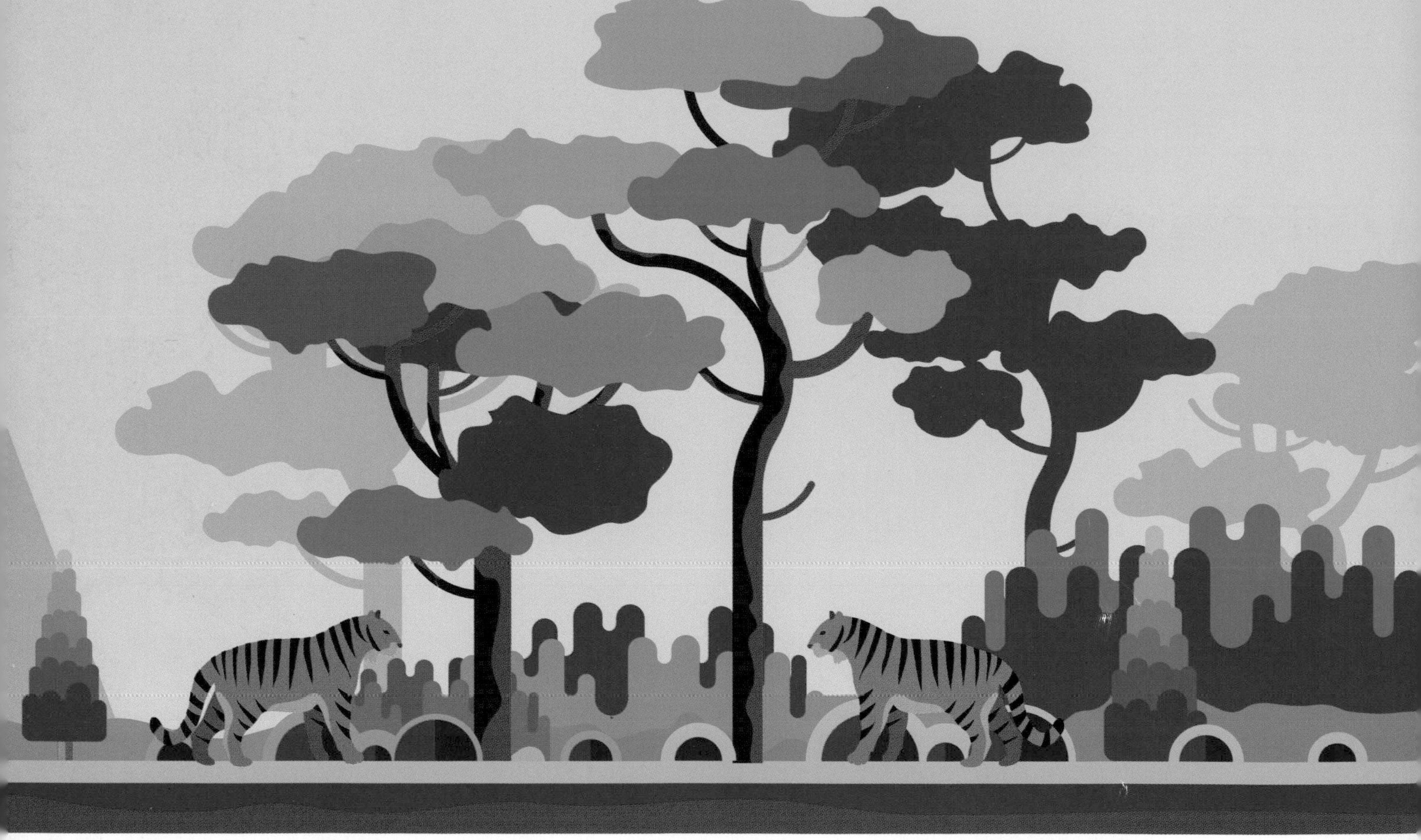

©2017
Book Life
King's Lynn
Norfolk PE30 4LS

ISBN: 978-1-78637-205-5

Written by:
Harriet Brundle

Edited by:
Charlie Ogden

Designed by:
Charlotte Neve

A catalogue record
for this book is
available from
the British Library.

# Habitats
## Infographics

# Contents

Words that are <u>underlined</u> are explained in the glossary on page 31.

# What Is a Habitat?

A living thing's habitat is the place where it naturally lives. Within a habitat, an animal might also have a home, for example a nest or a burrow.

Nest

Burrow

In order to survive, every animal needs a habitat that has food, water, air and shelter. Their habitat also needs to provide them with a safe place to raise their young.

If a habitat isn't meeting all the needs of the animals that live in it, the animals must move to a new habitat or risk dying out.

Rainforest

Pond

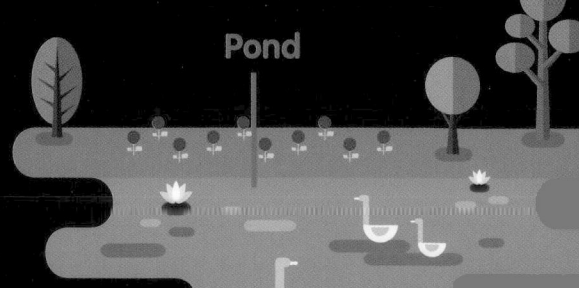

There are many different types of habitat around the world. Some habitats cover hundreds of kilometres and others could almost fit into the palm of your hand.

Some animals, such as tigers, prefer large habitats in which they can <u>roam</u>. Other animals, such as woodlice, are happy living alongside other <u>species</u>.

Each habitat is slightly different. Although they might look similar, two rivers will probably experience different types of weather, be different depths and flow at different speeds.

These differences make some habitats better suited to a particular animal's or plant's needs. For this reason, each habitat is home to a different combination of animal and plant species.

A small part of a habitat, which has different conditions to the rest of the habitat, is called a micro-habitat. For example, animals that live under rocks experience different conditions to those that live on top of the rocks. Because of this, these animals could be said to be living in a micro-habitat.

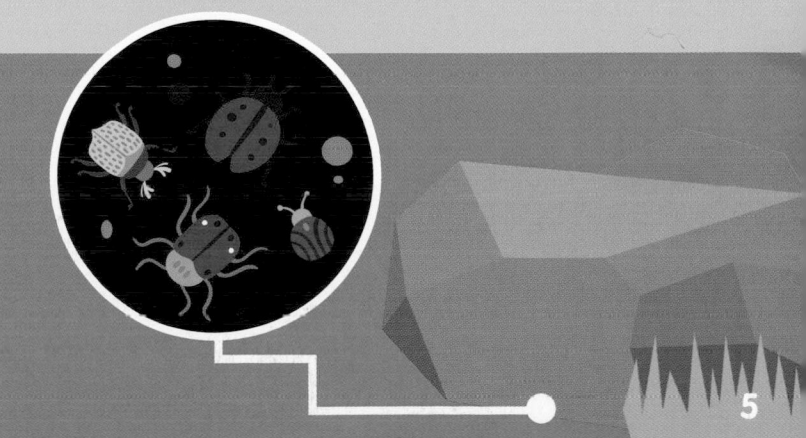

# Evolution and Adaptation

Evolution is the scientific concept that explains how all life on Earth developed from the first forms of life.

The gradual process by which single-celled <u>organisms</u> <u>multiplied</u> to create the different species of animal that we know today is an important part of evolution.

Evolution causes the <u>characteristics</u> of a species to change and these changes are then passed down through the <u>generations</u>.

In **1859,** after years of research, a man called Charles Darwin wrote a book that exposed the world to the idea of evolution.

Darwin visited the **Galapagos Islands** as part of his research.

Darwin believed that over a very long period of time, every species would naturally change in order to become better suited to their habitat. This long process of change is called **adaptation**.

Some lizards have long legs and others have shorter legs.

The lizards with long legs find it easier to climb trees to find food and escape <u>predators</u>.

Lizards with long legs will be more likely to live long enough to reproduce and their offspring will likely be born with long legs as well.

Lizards with short legs are more likely to die out because they cannot find food or escape from predators as easily.

Eventually, all the lizards in the species will have long legs.

Every species has adapted over time to become better suited to its habitat.

**Polar Bear:**
thick fur to keep it warm in cold weather.

**Cape Ground Squirrel:**
large, bushy tail to shade itself from the desert heat.

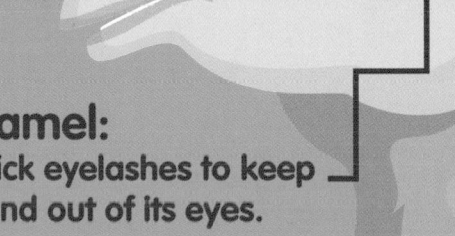

**Camel:**
thick eyelashes to keep sand out of its eyes.

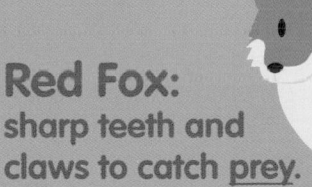

**Red Fox:**
sharp teeth and claws to catch <u>prey</u>.

# Changing Habitats

Habitats don't stay the same. Every habitat experiences daily changes, such as day and night, as well as long-term seasonal changes.

## Winter

In this time of year, the weather becomes much colder, meaning that plants, trees and grasses often die. In some places, these plants get covered by a thick layer of snow and ice, making it so that animals cannot reach them. Food in general becomes harder to find in winter. Some animals go into hibernation and are not seen again until spring. Many animals, especially birds, leave their habitats and migrate to warmer habitats during the colder months.

## Spring

There begins to be more hours of sunshine in the springtime. This helps the growth of grass and plant life. This growth attracts animals, especially insects. Animals that hibernated over the winter come out of hibernation and are ready to begin eating. Animals that migrated to warmer habitats for the winter begin to return to their normal habitats. A lot of animals raise young during the spring.

## Summer

The warmest and driest weather usually occurs in the summertime. During the summer, some places become so dry and warm that grasses and plants die. Water often becomes more difficult to find. In polar regions, large areas of sea ice melt during the summer, which reduces the size of the habitat considerably. Animals that migrate or hibernate eat as much as possible during this time in order to fatten themselves up in preparation for winter.

## Autumn

The weather begins to become colder and windier during the autumn. Many trees lose their leaves, which fall to the ground and provide food for animals such as worms. Animals that migrate will be getting prepared for their long journey to avoid the winter. Some animals begin hibernation in autumn, as much of the natural food supply begins to run out.

Not every habitat experiences the effects of these four seasons.

Deserts are extremely hot and humid and have little plant life all year round.

Some habitats experience a more permanent type of change. For example, they might be destroyed to make way for new roads or houses. This is called habitat destruction.

Find out more about habitat destruction on page 26.

# 8000 km

Humpback whales travel up to 8000 km during their migration.

# Ecosystems

Every habitat is home to a different group of animals and plants that all <u>interact</u> with each other. These living things also interact with non-living parts of the environment, such as the weather. This is called an ecosystem.

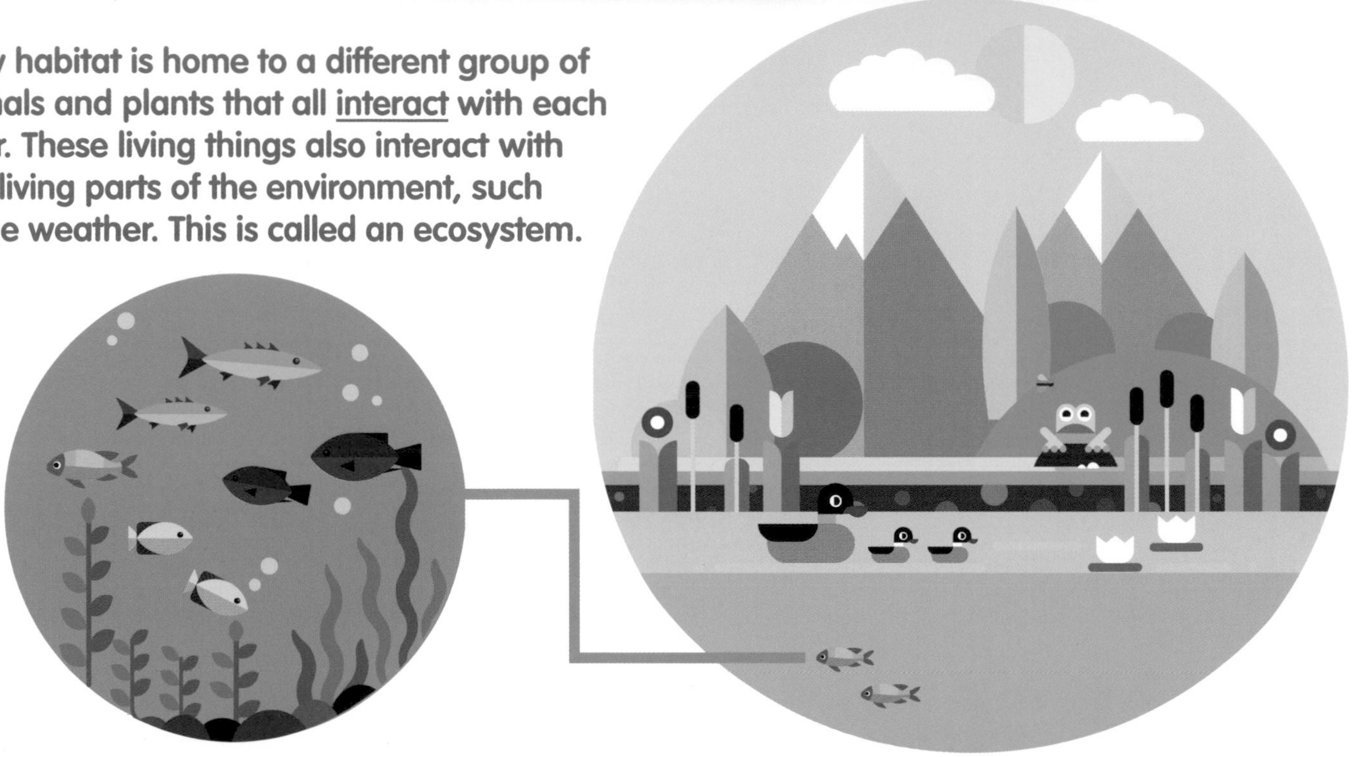

A healthy ecosystem relies upon energy being passed between different living things. Usually, energy is passed from plants, which are called producers, to small animals and then from these small animals to larger species of animal. This process is called a food chain.

| Grass | Antelope | Lion | Plant | Insect | Frog |

**Phytoplankton**  **Fish**  **Seal**  **Killer Whale**

The animals and plants in an ecosystem rely on each other, meaning that it is important that an ecosystem remains stable and does not dramatically change in a short amount of time. In a thriving ecosystem, all plants and animals have access to the things they need in order to survive.

If something happens to the plants in a habitat, the herbivores in that habitat could die out or be forced to move to a different habitat. If this happens, the carnivores in the food chain will also be affected, as they will no longer have herbivores to hunt. This shows how changing one part of an ecosystem can lead to the entire ecosystem being destroyed.

Ecosystems are damaged and destroyed for a number of different reasons, including:

**Drought**    **Extreme Heat**    **Natural Disasters**    **Human Behaviour**

Some habitats are able to grow back after they have been damaged. However, other habitats remain permanently destroyed and their ecosystems never recover.

11

# Rainforests

A rainforest is an extremely tall and dense forest that receives a lot of rain.

There are two types of rainforest:
1) Tropical
2) Temperate

Tropical rainforests are found in warm and wet areas near to the Equator. They experience much higher temperatures than temperate rainforests.

Equator

Temperate rainforests are found farther from the Equator and nearer to the polar regions. They experience cooler temperatures than tropical rainforests.

**Amazon Rainforest**

The largest tropical rainforest in the world is the Amazon rainforest in South America. It is home to millions of different animal and plant species and is over 5.5 million kilometres in size!

South America

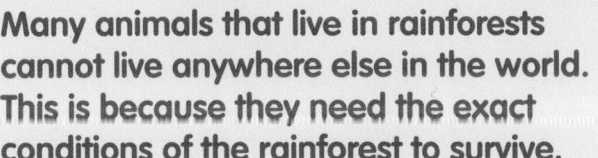

Many animals that live in rainforests cannot live anywhere else in the world. This is because they need the exact conditions of the rainforest to survive.

# Rainforests have four layers:

**Emergent Layer** – The very tallest trees grow into the emergent layer and receive plenty of sunlight. These trees are usually home to animals such as eagles, bats and small monkeys. Trees in the emergent layer of the rainforest can be up to 70 metres tall!

**Canopy Layer** – At this level, the trees are packed closely together and their leaves form a dense roof over the rainforest. There is plenty of food in this layer. Because of this, the trees are home to a wide range of animals including tree frogs, birds and sloths.

**Understory** – This layer is made up of small trees and plants. The area receives little sunlight as it is shaded by the canopy layer. Rain drips through the canopy, meaning that the understory is damp. Animals such as jaguars, snakes and leopards live in the understory.

**Forest Floor** – This area is dark and damp because it receives little sunlight. As a result, plant and animal remains <u>decompose</u> very quickly down here. Small organisms feed on the remains. This is the start of the food chain in the rainforest. Animals such as tapirs, gorillas and tigers also live on the forest floor.

**Different animals use the layers of the rainforest in different ways:**
Eagles sit on the highest branches in the emergent layer, looking for their prey. Smaller animals hide under the large leaves of the shrubs in the understory to avoid being seen by predators, such as eagles.

## 10 Minutes

It can take as long as 10 minutes for a drop of rain to travel through the canopy and reach the rainforest floor!

# Deserts

A desert is an extremely barren area of land that experiences very little rainfall and very high temperatures.

These difficult conditions make the desert a very <u>hostile</u> environment for animals and plants to live in. Carnivores must work hard to find and catch enough prey to sustain them, while herbivores search tirelessly for the little plant life that can grow in the desert.

Due to the lack of water, the high temperatures and the lack of food, many species have had to adapt in order to survive in desert habitats.

The cape ground squirrel has a large fluffy tail, which it can lift above its head to shade itself from the heat of the Sun.

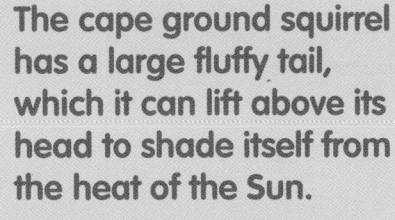
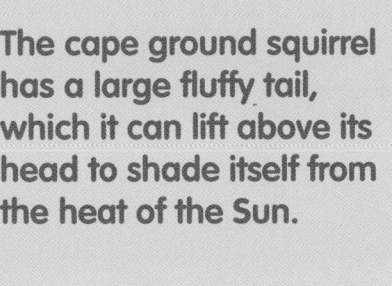

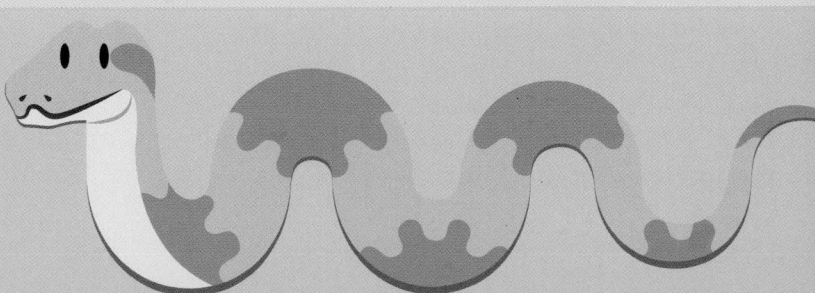

The thorny devil dragon has spikes on its body that channel <u>condensation</u> from the animal's body into the corners of its mouth.

The sidewinder snake moves with part of its body in the air. This means that less of its body is touching the extremely hot desert sand.

# Over 100 miles

The sandgrouse bird flies over 100 miles each day to find a desert watering hole. Once there, it soaks its feathers in the water. The bird then carries the water in its feathers back to its thirsty chicks.

Many desert animals choose to stay in the shade during the hottest part of the day.

The horned viper snake buries itself underneath the top layer of sand in order to reach the cooler sand below. It leaves just its nostrils poking out so that it can still breathe.

The deathstalker scorpion hides in cracks in rocks during the day and comes out at night to hunt.

Dorcas gazelles hide in the shade during the hottest part of the day, only coming out early in the morning and late at night to feed.

**The Sahara desert** is the largest desert in the world. Found in Africa, it is over 9 million km² in size. During the daytime, temperatures in the Sahara can reach above 40 °C.

At night, the temperatures in deserts can drop dramatically, even falling below **0 °C.**

# Oceans

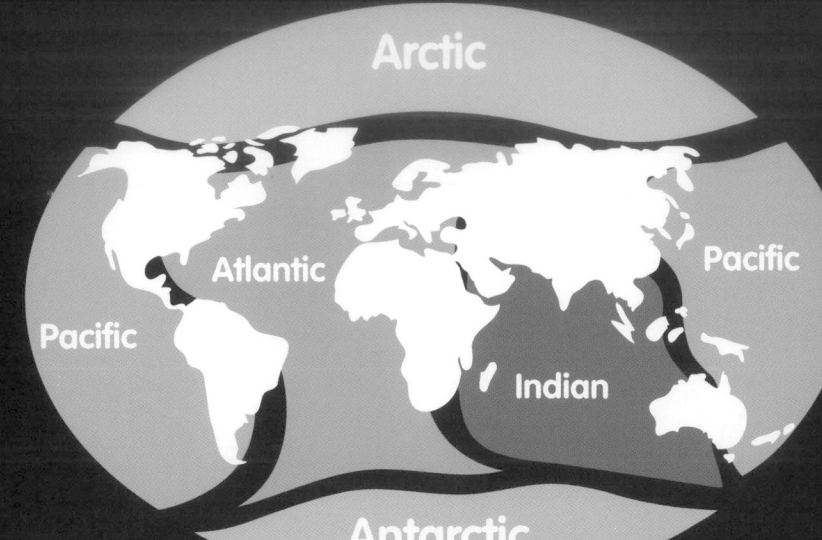

Arctic

Pacific

Atlantic

Pacific

Indian

Antarctic

Our Earth has five large bodies of water called oceans, as well as several smaller seas.

The oceans are home to some of the biggest, fastest, scariest and best-camouflaged animals in the world.

**The five oceans are called:**
1) Pacific Ocean
2) Atlantic Ocean
3) Indian Ocean
4) Arctic Ocean
5) Antarctic Ocean
(also known as the Southern Ocean)

Great White Shark

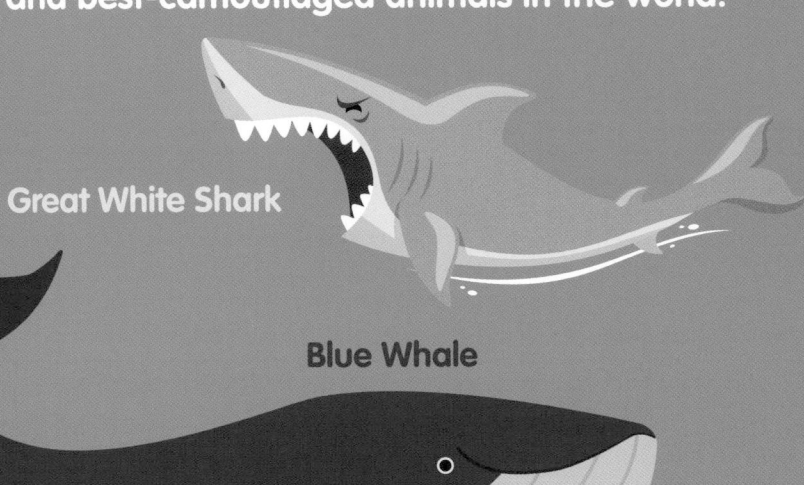

Blue Whale

Over **70%** of the Earth's surface is covered in water.

## 25 metres

Sailfish

Tasselled Anglerfish

## 68 mph

Some animals spend part of their life in the ocean and part of their life on land. Seagoing iguanas live on <u>volcanic</u> islands, but dive into the sea for up to 30 minutes at a time to eat the vegetation on the sea floor.

An increasing number of ocean species, including whales, sharks and sea turtles, are now classed as <u>endangered</u> animals.

Oceans are the largest habitats in the world and they are home to very complicated ecosystems.

Phytoplankton, seaweed and seagrasses live on the sea floor.

Small carnivores, such as sardines, eat the small herbivores.

Small herbivores, such as sea urchins, eat the plant life.

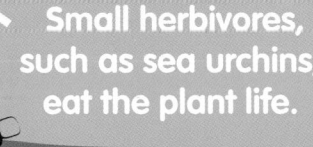

Top predators, such as sharks, eat the small carnivores.

**Cold** oceans tend to be rich in oxygen and nutrients, which feed the producers at the bottom of the food chain. This means that cold oceans often support large quantities of a small number of species.

**Warmer** oceans are home to a wider range of species, but smaller numbers of each species, as there is less vegetation to support the food chain.

Animals use the conditions in their habitat to help them survive. Most seals prefer the cold water and sea ice in the Antarctic Ocean. The cold water attracts prey, such as penguins, meaning that the seals can rest on the ice while they wait for their prey to come close.

The ocean is home to the world's largest living structure: the **Great Barrier Reef** off the coast of Australia. An estimated 10% of the world's fish species live around the Great Barrier Reef.

Six different species of sea turtle come to the reef to breed. Larger animals such as whales, dolphins and <u>porpoises</u> also live on the reef.

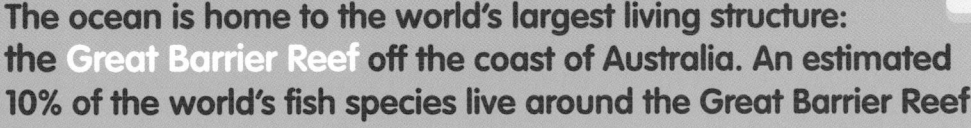
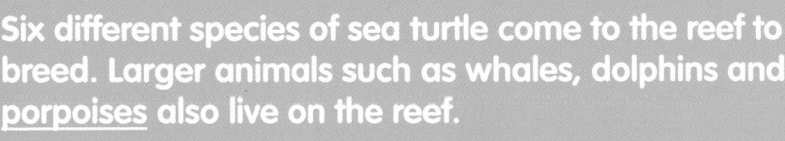

# Grasslands

Grasslands are large, open areas of land that are covered in different grasses. Grasslands don't experience enough rain to support large amounts of trees.

The grasses and plants that grow in grassland areas are able to continue growing even after they have been partly eaten by grazing animals, which makes these areas a suitable habitat for large numbers of herbivores.

Grasslands are home to <u>herds</u> of animals that graze on plant life. These herbivores share the grasslands with the carnivores that hunt them. Smaller animals, such as snakes, mice and rabbits, also live in the grasslands and use the grass to hide from predators. Birds use the wide open spaces to search for prey from the sky.

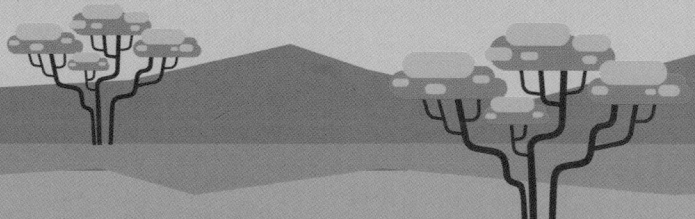

A savannah, or a tropical grassland, is a type of grassland that is found in warm <u>climates</u>. Savannahs usually have more trees than other grasslands. It is estimated that nearly **50%** of Africa is covered by savannahs.

In the summertime, savannahs experience heavy rains. In the dry season, there is very little rainfall.

The plants in tropical grasslands have adapted to survive the dry seasons. They have long roots that can reach water deep underground and stems that can store the water for long periods of time.

Roots

The Serengeti Plains are a tropical grassland. They are home to herds of animals such as wildebeest, zebra and antelope. These animals spend their days moving around and grazing on the grass. Animals such as lions, leopards and cheetahs also live on the plains and hunt the herbivores.

Due to the lack of rainfall in grasslands, different species often all gather around the same watering hole for a much-needed drink. These areas often become quite a spectacle, as lots of animals from countless different species can all descend upon on a large watering hole at the same time.

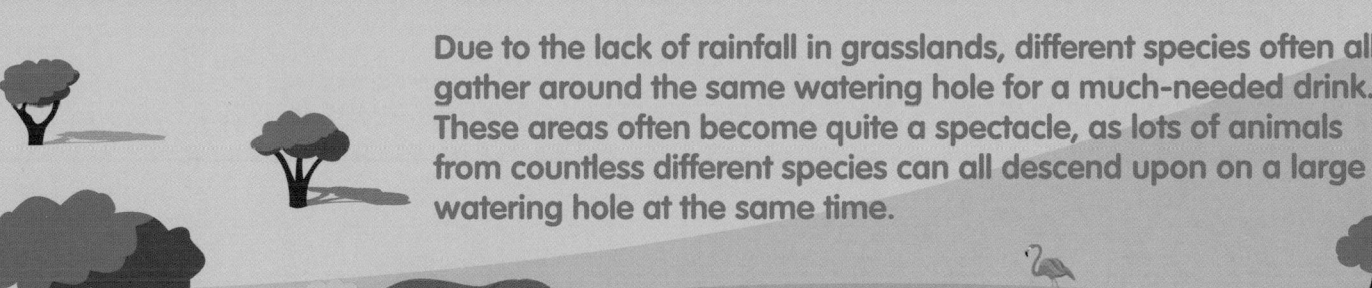

Other grasslands are known as temperate grasslands. One type of temperate grassland is known as a prairie. These areas experience cooler temperatures and are home to animals such as buffalo, deer and rabbit.

North Dakota — South Dakota

Nebraska —

United States of America

Prairies

Texas —

If <u>overgrazing</u> happens on grasslands, the vegetation cannot re-grow and the area becomes a desert. Large areas of savannah are lost to the Sahara desert in this way each year.

# Mountains

Mountains are the largest landforms on Earth. They are steeper and higher than hills and are formed by movements in the Earth's <u>crust</u>.

Mountain habitats can be extremely hard to survive in. They offer a range of different challenges for the animals that live there, including a lack of food, cold temperatures and steep, rocky slopes.

Mountains often have micro-climates, where different parts of the same mountain have very different conditions from one another.

**1.** The top part of a mountain has the coldest temperatures and, in some cases, is covered in snow. There is often very little oxygen in the air at this level, which makes it extremely difficult for plants and animals to survive. The soil is also very thin here, making it even more difficult for plants to grow.

**2.** As you move farther down the mountain, the air gets less thin and begins to contain more oxygen. As a result, there are more trees, plants and animals living here.

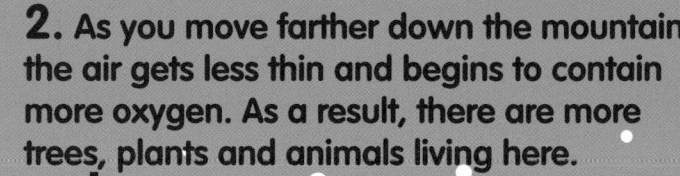

**3.** The lowest part of the mountain can usually support the most life as the temperature is warmer. The lower <u>altitude</u> means that there is more oxygen in the air. Because of this, these areas can usually support a range of trees, plants and animals.

Due to the extreme environment, animals living on mountains have had to adapt to survive.

Mountain goats can be found on the steep slopes of mountains in North America.

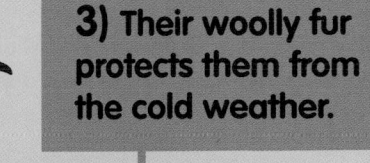
**3) Their woolly fur protects them from the cold weather.**

**1) They have eight front teeth, which helps them to grab large mouthfuls of grass at a time.**

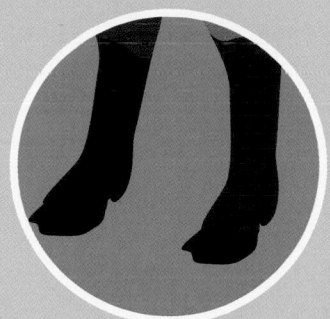

**2) They have curved, flexible hooves that help them to balance on the steep mountainside.**

The Rocky Mountains are found in the U.S.A. and Canada. They are made up of around 100 smaller <u>mountain ranges.</u> The Rocky Mountains are home to a vast range of different habitats such as forests, tundras, rivers and prairies.

These habitats support huge numbers of animals:

**1.** Large mammals, such as grizzly bears and mountain lions, prowl the mountains looking for prey.

**2.** Sheep and mountain goats live at higher altitudes during the summertime and move to lower parts of the mountain during the colder winter months.

**3.** Beavers, river otters, frogs and salamanders can be found in and around the rivers flowing through the mountain range.

## Did You Know?

Grizzly bears in the Rocky Mountains use large trees as scratching posts! The bears rub their backs up and down against the trees. Scientists think they do this to scratch an itch or to leave their <u>scent</u> on the tree.

# Emerging Habitats

In the last 100 years, the population on Earth has risen by over four billion people.

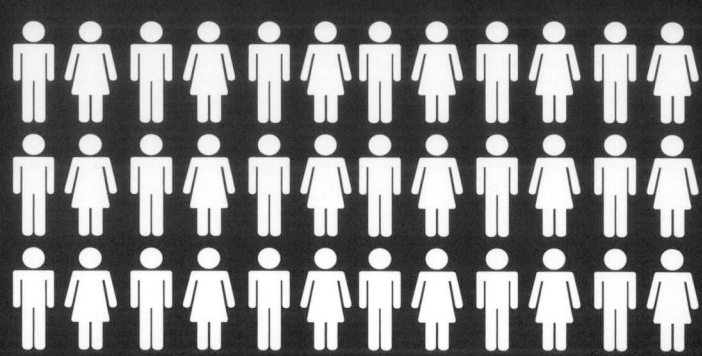

Every one of those people needs space to live in. As a result, large areas of land that used to be home to wildlife have been destroyed to make way for new homes. In the last 50 years, nearly 20% of the Amazon rainforest has been cut down. That's an area around the size of France!

All these people also need food to eat. Every year, habitats are destroyed to make space for <u>livestock</u> and crops.

As huge areas of land have become <u>urbanised</u>, many animals have been unable to adapt to the new, busy environment. These animals have been forced to move to new habitats.

However, some animals, such as rats and cockroaches, have thrived in these new environments. These animals tend to be good <u>scavengers</u>, feeding on the waste that is produced by humans.

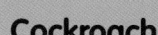
Cockroach

Coyotes are now living in many cities in America. These animals survive on food waste left behind by humans.

Langur monkeys have learnt to live on the rooftops of buildings in Jodhpur, India. They use the height of the rooftops to look for opportunities to steal food from markets and the people living in the city.

In Mumbai, leopards prey on the livestock owned by people living on the outskirts of the city. The leopards use the noise of the busy city to their advantage. It hides any noise they might make as they approach their prey.

In Singapore, man-made 'supertrees', which can be up to 50 metres tall, have been put up in the middle of the city. The structures are covered in plant life and are connected to each other by high-up walkways.

**Mumbai**

**Singapore**

Animals are beginning to move into the new urban habitats that are expanding across the world. Because of this, it's important that we all try to look after the animals in our local area.

**Over half** of the world's population now lives in urban areas.

# Extreme Adaptations

Due to the extreme nature of certain habitats, some animals have had to adapt in weird and wonderful ways just to survive.

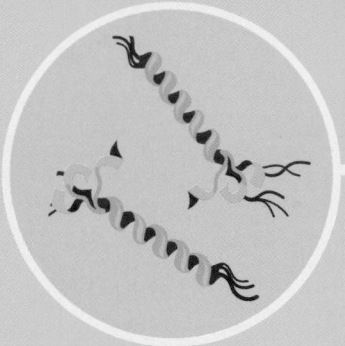

**Antifreeze Protein**

−2°C

Arctic fish live in extremely cold waters. It has recently been discovered that these fish have an antifreeze protein in their blood that prevents harmful ice crystals forming inside their bodies.

The sword-billed hummingbird has an extremely long beak. This allows it to reach into large flowers, which are too big for other birds, and drink the nectar within!

The sword-billed hummingbird is the only bird to have a beak that is longer than its body!

The Spanish ribbed newt can force its ribs through its chest and use them to protect itself from predators. Once the predator has moved on, the newt's ribs move back inside its body and the skin quickly heals over.

Hippopotamuses are known to sweat a bright red <u>substance</u> that looks like blood. The substance helps to protect the animal's skin from the burning heat of the Sun. It also helps to stop bacteria from growing and causing skin infections.

The mimic octopus has adapted to be able to copy the shape, colour and texture of other animals. This means that it can make itself look like a predator to avoid being hunted as prey!

The sperm whale has adapted to be able to store huge amounts of oxygen in its blood. This allows the whale to hold its breath for a long time, meaning that it can dive deep into the ocean to search for food.

The Texas horned lizard has disgusting tasting blood! When it's attacked, it shoots blood straight from its eye, giving the predator a taste it won't enjoy.

# Habitat Destruction

Habitat destruction is when a habitat becomes unable to support the species living in it because the area has changed or been destroyed. As a result, the animals that lived in the habitat can find it very difficult to survive.

Both human and natural activity can be responsible for habitat destruction.

Natural causes of habitat destruction include:

**Fires**

**Diseases**

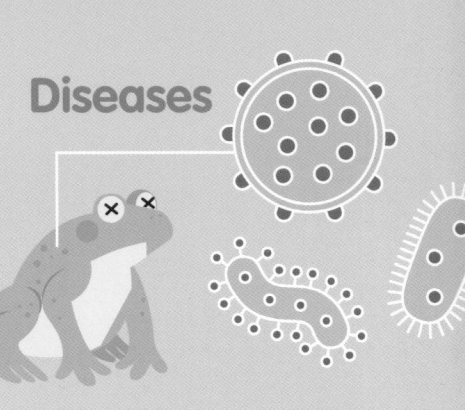

**Floods**

**Volcanic Activity**

**Earthquakes**

Human causes of habitat destruction include:

## 1) Pollution

Pollution is the introduction of a harmful substance into an environment. One type of pollution is called acid rain. Acid rain is made when harmful gases build up in Earth's <u>atmosphere</u> and combine with rain water. When acid rain falls on forests, it can strip the trees of their leaves and kill plant life. Without producers in the food chain, the entire ecosystem could be destroyed.

## 2) Climate Change

Climate change is the result of a process called global warming. Humans use energy for lots of different reasons, such as powering our cars and heating our homes. This energy is largely produced by burning <u>fossil fuels</u>, like coal, gas and oil. When these fuels are burnt, they release gases known as greenhouse gases.

Layers of Gases

The Earth's atmosphere is the collection of different gases that surround the planet. These gases allow light and heat from the Sun to pass through to Earth. Some of this heat bounces off our planet and escapes back through the atmosphere and into space.

Greenhouse gases mix with Earth's atmosphere. These gases do not allow heat to pass back through the atmosphere, meaning that the heat becomes trapped on Earth. As a result, the temperature on Earth is rising. The more greenhouse gases that are produced, the faster global warming happens.

These warmer temperatures are responsible for changing habitats all around the world. One example of this is the melting ice in polar regions. The melting ice in these places reduces the size of the habitat available for the animals that live there. Animals such as polar bears and seals, which rely on the sea ice to hunt, will find life increasingly difficult as the ice in their habitat continues to melt.

## 3) Deforestation

This is when trees are cut down in very large numbers, often to make room for buildings and farms. Deforestation is happening all over the world and at an extremely fast rate. Many animals cannot survive the immediate loss of habitat that deforestation causes. Around 50% of the world's forests have been destroyed and are continuing to be destroyed at a rate faster than they can re-grow.

## 4) Overfishing

Overfishing occurs when more fish are caught and removed from the sea than can be naturally replaced through reproduction. As a result, some species of fish, for example bluefin tuna, are now a threatened species and some ecosystems are damaged beyond repair.

Millions of <u>tonnes</u> of rubbish are dumped into the ocean every year.

# Habitat Protection

There are lots of different people and organisations around the world who try to protect animal habitats.

Organisations such as The World Wide Fund for Nature (WWF) and Greenpeace work hard to make sure that habitats are protected, whilst also campaigning to try to reduce global pollution and climate change.

## The World Wide Fund for Nature (WWF)
was established in 1961. The organisation works in over 100 countries and has millions of supporters, making it the largest of its type in the world.

WWF focusses on six key areas: safeguarding wildlife, protecting oceans and forests, creating sustainable timber and seafood sources, reducing climate change and encouraging every person to do their part to help.

Some parks and reserves offer the opportunity for visitors to pay money to see the animals living there. This money helps towards maintaining the habitat.

National parks have been established worldwide to offer a safe place for animals to live. These areas are protected by law, meaning that they cannot be damaged by human activity.

## The Great Barrier Reef
has also been protected by laws, meaning that humans cannot fish or take plant life from that part of the ocean.

Alaska

### Denali National Park and Preserve
is 24,000 km$^2$ in size and offers a protected habitat for animals such as grizzly bears, caribou and wolves.

# What Can We Do?

1. Try to find out about the habitats in your local area and consider becoming involved with local conservation groups.

2. Try not to be wasteful. Food production is a major reason for habitat destruction, so try not to waste fresh food.

3. Tell your family and friends all about how important it is to look after animals and their habitats.

4. Ask if you can put up bird feeders at home or at school. Try to protect the animals in your local area by not dropping litter on the ground.

## 2.8 million supporters

Greenpeace started in 1971 and it now has around 2.8 million supporters from all over the world.

# Activity

Make a list of all the different habitats you have seen in your local area. Do you have any woodland areas nearby? Or is there a pond, river or lake that you could visit?

Think about all the different animals that might live in those different habitats. In what ways are they well-suited to their habitat?

Now think about a habitat that is totally different to your local area. What sort of animals live there? Why might they differ from the animals that live in habitats near you?

# Glossary

**altitude** the height of an object in relation to sea level or ground level

**atmosphere** the mixture of gases that make up the air and surround the Earth

**carnivores** animals that eat other animals rather than plants

**characteristics** features of a thing that help to identify it

**climates** the common weather conditions in certain places

**condensation** water that collects as droplets on a surface

**crust** the outermost layer of Earth

**decompose** decay or rot

**endangered** when a species of animal is in danger of going extinct

**Equator** the imaginary line around the Earth that is an equal distance from the North and South Pole

**fossil fuels** fuels, such as coal, oil and gas, that formed millions of years ago from the remains of animals and plants

**generations** animals from the same species that are roughly the same age

**herbivores** animals that only eat plants

**herds** large groups of animals that live together

**hibernation** the process of spending the winter sleeping or in a dormant state

**hostile** very unfriendly

**interact** communicate and have an effect on each other

**livestock** animals that are kept for farming purposes

**migrate** move from one place to another based on seasonal changes

**mountain ranges** groups of connected mountains

**multiplied** increased in number or quantity

**nectar** a sweet liquid made by flowers in order to attract insects

**organisms** individual plants or animals

**overgrazing** grazing so heavily that the vegetation gets damaged and may not grow back

**phytoplankton** plankton consisting of microscopic plants

**polar regions** areas surrounding the North and South Poles

**porpoises** small-toothed whales with rounded snouts

**predators** animals that hunt other animals for food

**prey** animals that are hunted by other animals for food

**protein** an organic compound that performs important roles in the body

**reproduce** to produce young through the act of mating

**roam** wander freely or aimlessly, often over a wide area

**scavengers** animals that feed on waste products or other animals that are already dead

**scent** a distinctive smell

**species** a group of very similar animals or plants that are capable of producing young together

**substance** something with physical properties

**sustainable** able to be maintained at a certain rate or level

**temperate** a region or climate that is characterised by mild temperatures

**tonnes** units of measurement that each equal one thousand kilograms

**urbanised** made to be more like a town or city by adding buildings and raising the population

**volcanic** relating to volcanoes

# Index